P9-AOP-690

Jackie Robinson

Published in the United States of America by Cherry Lake Publishing
Ann Arbor, Michigan
www.cherrylakepublishing.com

Content Adviser: Ryan Emery Hughes, Doctoral Student, School of Education, University of Michigan
Reading Adviser: Marla Conn MS, Ed., Literacy specialist, Read-Ability, Inc.
Book Design: Jennifer Wahi
Illustrator: Jeff Bane

Photo Credits: © Hulton Archive/Getty Images, 5; © National Baseball Hall of Fame Library, Cooperstown, New York, 7, 13, 15, 23; © Afro American Newspapers/Gado/Getty Images, 9, 22; © Negro League Baseball Museum, 11; © Everett Collection Inc / Alamy Stock Photo, 17; © ZUMA Press Inc / Alamy Stock Photo, 19; © U.S. Information Agency/NARA, 21; Cover, 6, 10, 16, Jeff Bane; Various frames throughout, Shutterstock Images

Copyright ©2017 by Cherry Lake Publishing
All rights reserved. No part of this book may be reproduced or utilized in any form or by any means without written permission from the publisher.

Library of Congress Cataloging-in-Publication Data

Names: Haldy, Emma E., author.
Title: Jackie Robinson / Emma E. Haldy.
Description: Ann Arbor : Cherry Lake Publishing, [2016] | Series: My
    Itty-Bitty Bio | Includes index.
Identifiers: LCCN 2015045598| ISBN 9781634710213 (hardcover) | ISBN
    9781634711203 (pdf) | ISBN 9781634712194 (paperback) | ISBN 9781634713184
    (ebook)
Subjects: LCSH: Robinson, Jackie, 1919-1972--Juvenile literature. | Baseball
    players--United States--Biography--Juvenile literature. | African American
    baseball players--Biography--Juvenile literature.
Classification: LCC GV865.R6 H35 2016 | DDC 796.357092--dc23
LC record available at http://lccn.loc.gov/2015045598

Printed in the United States of America
Corporate Graphics

About the author: Emma E. Haldy is a former librarian and a proud Michigander. She lives with her husband, Joe, and an ever-growing collection of books.

About the illustrator: Jeff Bane and his two business partners own a studio along the American River in Folsom, California, home of the 1849 Gold Rush. When Jeff's not sketching or illustrating for clients, he's either swimming or kayaking in the river to relax.

I was born in 1919.

I had four brothers and sisters. We were raised by a single mom.

When were you born?

I was good at sports. I played football. I played baseball.

I briefly went to college. I served in the Army.

I fell in love with Rachel Isum.
We got married.

We had three children.

I was playing baseball **professionally**. But baseball was **segregated**.

I could not play with white people. I could only play with black people.

The owner of the Dodgers wanted to change things.
He hired me.

I became the first black player in the major leagues. I wore the number 42.

Many people were mad.
They yelled at me. They tried
to scare me. They threw things
at me.

But I knew I had to be strong.
I did not give up. I showed them
I could play.

Why do you think people
were so mean?

I won Rookie of the Year.

I played for nine more years.
We won **championships**.
We won a World Series.

Baseball had **integrated**. There were no more black teams. There were no more white teams.

I was proud. I had made an impact.

I worked to help others until my death in 1972.

I was a respected man.
I overcame hate. I changed baseball forever.

What would you like to ask me?

1946

1910

Born
1919

1947

2010

Died
1972

glossary

championships (CHAM-pee-uhn-ships) final games of the year that pick the overall winner

integrated (IN-tuh-gray-tid) not separated by race

professionally (pruh-FESH-uh-nuhl-ee) getting paid

segregated (SEG-ri-gay-tid) separated by race

index